The Life of
H. J. Heinz

M. C. Hall

Heinemann
LIBRARY

SPRING COTTAGE
PRIMARY SCHOOL

www.heinemann.co.uk/library

To order:
- Phone 44 (0) 1865 888066
- Send a fax to 44 (0) 1865 314091
- Visit the Heinemann Bookshop at www.heinemann.co.uk/library to browse our catalogue and order online.

First published in Great Britain by Heinemann Library, Halley Court, Jordan Hill, Oxford OX2 8EJ, part of Harcourt Education.
Heinemann is a registered trademark of Harcourt Education Ltd.

© Harcourt Education Ltd 2003
First published in paperback in 2004.
The moral right of the proprietor has been asserted.

All rights reserved. No part of this publication may be reproduced, stored in a retrieval system, or transmitted in any form or by any means, electronic, mechanical, photocopying, recording, or otherwise, without either the prior written permission of the Publishers or a licence permitting restricted copying in the United Kingdom issued by the Copyright Licensing Agency Ltd, 90 Tottenham Court Road, London W1T 4LP (www.cla.co.uk).

Editorial: Angela McHaney Brown, Kathy Peltan
Design: Herman Adler Design
Illustrations: Robert Lawson
Picture Research: Carol Parden
Production: Edward Moore

Originated by QueNet™
Printed and bound in China by South China Printing Company

ISBN 0 431 18071 7 (hardback)
07 06 05 04 03
10 9 8 7 6 5 4 3 2 1

ISBN 0 431 18076 8 (paperback)
07 06 05 04
10 9 8 7 6 5 4 3 2 1

British Library Cataloguing in Publication Data
Hall, M. C.
 The Life of H. J. Heinz
 338.7'664'092

A full catalogue record for this book is available from the British Library.

Acknowledgements

The Publishers would like to thank the following for permission to reproduce photographs: pp. 5C, 20, 22, 25 Library & Archives/Historical Society of Western Pennsylvania, Pittsburgh; p. 5L icon Comstock; p. 6 Directory of Pittsburgh & Allegheny Cities, J. F. Diffenbach, Publisher/Pittsburgh History & Landmark Foundation; p. 9 Eric Chrichton/Corbis; pp. 10, 11 Henry Ford Museum & Greenfield Village; pp. 12, 13, 14, 15, 17, 18, 19, 21, 23, 27 H. J. Heinz Company; p. 24 Culver Pictures; p. 26 The Carnegie Library, Pittsburgh; p. 28 Heinz Family Archives; p. 29 Heinz Hitch

Cover photographs by Brian Warling/Heinemann Library and Henry Ford Museum & Greenfield Village.

Special thanks to Michelle Rimsa for her comments in the preparation of this book.

Disclaimer
All the Internet addresses (URLs) given in this book were valid at the time of going to press. However, due to the dynamic nature of the Internet, some addresses may have changed, or sites may have changed or ceased to exist since publication. While the author and the Publishers regret any inconvenience this may cause readers, no responsibility for any such changes can be accepted by either the author or the Publishers.

Contents

Food in packages 4
The early years 6
Selling vegetables 8
Business ideas 10
Hard times and a fresh start 12
A new kind of factory 14
Making good food 16
Making food safe to eat 18
Spreading the word 20
Success in business 22
Helping others 24
Later life 26
Learning more about Heinz 28
Fact file 30
Timeline 30
Glossary 31
More books to read 31
Index 32

Any words in bold, **like this**, are explained in the Glossary

Food in packages

Today, many people buy **processed** foods that are ready to eat. These foods are sold in boxes, bags, tins and bottles.

The Heinz Company makes many different products.

H. J. Heinz started one of the first companies that made processed foods. He wanted his foods to be **nutritious**. He also wanted them to taste good and to be safe to eat.

By the time he was in his 40s, Heinz was a famous man.

The early years

Henry John Heinz was born in 1844 in Birmingham, Pennsylvania, USA. His parents called him Harry. When Harry was five, the family moved to the nearby town of Sharpsburg.

Harry's father started a **brickyard**. There were other companies like it at that time, such as Kier Brothers.

Harry's mother had a large kitchen garden. Harry helped in the garden and brickyard. He also sold vegetables to his neighbours. Harry's parents gave him a vegetable garden of his own so he could grow more.

Harry liked working in the garden.

Selling vegetables

When he was twelve, Harry bought a horse and cart so could travel further to sell his vegetables. He started selling a spicy **horseradish** sauce. Harry and his mother made it themselves.

Harry often went to the nearest big city, Pittsburgh, to sell vegetables and sauces.

Harry used fresh horseradish for his sauces.

Some people mixed turnips with horseradish so it cost less to make. Harry did not think this was right. He put his pure horseradish in clear bottles. That way people could see what they were buying.

Business ideas

Harry continued to work in the **brickyard**. He had the idea of using machines to heat and dry the bricks. That meant the brickyard did not need to close during cold weather.

When he was still a young man, Harry bought part of his father's business.

However, Harry was more interested in selling food. When he was 25, he and a friend started a company called Anchor Brand Foods. Bottled **horseradish** was their first **product**.

Anchor Brand Foods was started in Harry's home in Sharpsburg.

Hard times and a fresh start

In 1869, Harry married Sarah Young. Sarah helped Harry with the business. However, Anchor Brand Foods had money problems. In 1875, the company had to close.

Harry and Sarah are shown here, on the left, with another couple.

Harry did not give up. He got his brother and cousin to start a business, then went to work there. In 1888, Harry bought it from them and named it the H. J. Heinz Company.

Some early Heinz **products** looked quite different from how they look today.

A new kind of factory

Harry's workers had a safe, clean place to work.

Harry built a **factory** in Allegheny, Pennsylvania. At the time, many factories were dirty and dangerous. Harry gave his **employees** better working conditions.

Harry also wanted his employees to learn things. His company offered free classes in subjects like sewing and music. The factory also had a restaurant, a hospital and a swimming pool.

Heinz **managers** had a rooftop garden to relax in.

Making good food

Some food **processing** companies used poor quality vegetables and fruit in their foods. Their **products** were not very **nutritious** and often tasted bad.

Harry used only fresh, high-quality vegetables and fruits in Heinz products.

Harry believed that processed food could taste good and also be nutritious. He worked with farmers to grow larger, better-tasting fruit and vegetables.

Heinz workers chose the best fruit and vegetables to put in each jar.

Making food safe to eat

Some companies added **chemicals** to food to keep it from rotting and making people ill. Harry knew that if food was **processed** correctly it would not go bad.

Harry did not want to use many chemicals in his foods, because the chemicals were not good for people.

Harry thought there should be rules about how food is processed. He worked hard to get the United States **government** to pass the Pure Food and Drug Act in 1906. This law has helped make American food safe.

By law, a food label has to list everything in the **product**.

Spreading the word

Harry had many ideas for **marketing** his **products**. He gave away free food samples. He also gave away badges shaped like pickles.

Everyone who wore a Heinz pickle badge helped spread the company name.

Harry also used a horse-drawn wagon to advertise his products.

Harry let people come to his **factory** to watch the workers. He also came up with the saying 'Heinz 57 Varieties'. The company had more than 57 products, but Harry liked the sound of the number.

Success in business

This picture shows the Heinz factory in Pittsburgh in about 1910.

Harry became rich and successful. He began to travel around the world. Harry often visited **factories** in other countries, looking for new ideas.

When he travelled, Harry bought paintings, clocks and other things he liked. He built a huge house in Pittsburgh. One floor of the house was a **museum** filled with his collections.

This is Harry's home, Greenlawn, photographed around 1919.

Helping others

Harry wanted to make Pittsburgh a better place to live. Most **factories** produced a smoke that made the air dirty and hard to breathe. The Heinz factory used special equipment that produced less smoke.

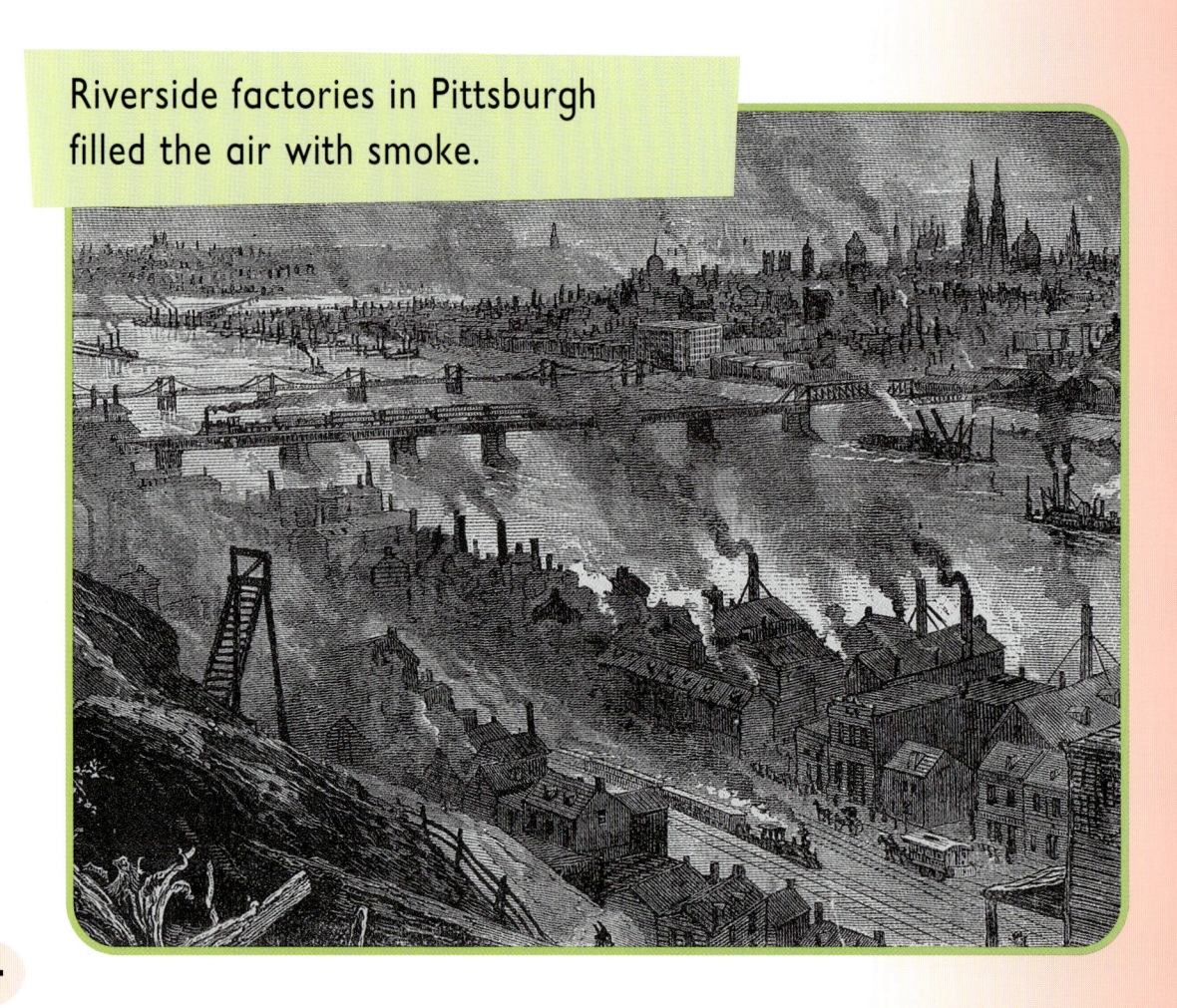

Riverside factories in Pittsburgh filled the air with smoke.

Sarah died in 1894. Some years later, Harry had a centre built for city children. He called it Sarah Heinz House. He also gave gifts to his home town, Sharpsburg, where he had started his first business.

The Sarah Heinz House had a swimming pool and many rooms for visiting children to use.

Later life

As he grew older, Harry spent time with his children and grandchildren. He wanted the world to be peaceful for all children. Harry visited other countries to talk to other people who were working for peace.

Harry and his grandchildren are shown here in front of one of his **greenhouses**.

Heinz was 74 when this photo was taken in 1918.

Even after he died in 1919, Harry Heinz continued to help others. He left some of his money to schools, hospitals, churches and groups that helped children.

Learning more about Heinz

People can learn about Harry Heinz by visiting Greenfield Village **Museum** in Dearborn, Michigan. The house in Sharpsburg in which Harry started his business was moved there in 1954.

Harry collected many beautiful things. The Carnegie Museum in Pittsburgh has a lot of artwork and watches from his collection.

This group of Heinz horses is going to a show.

Huge horses like the ones that once pulled Heinz Company wagons still appear at fairs and parades. Today people can still buy Heinz **products** in shops around the world.

Fact file

- Pickles became one of the Heinz company's best-selling **products**. In fact, H. J. Heinz was known as the 'Pickle King'.
- The H. J. Heinz Company **factory** became world famous for being a good place to work.
- In 1898, Harry Heinz built the Heinz Ocean Pier in Atlantic City, New Jersey. The pier was torn down after a bad storm in 1944.
- The horses that pulled the Heinz Company wagons were treated well. There was even a garden where the animals could walk.

Timeline

1844	Henry John (Harry) Heinz is born
1856	Harry buys a horse and cart to use for selling vegetables
1869	Harry and a friend start Anchor Brand Foods; Harry marries Sarah Young
1876	Harry's brother and cousin start the F. & J. Heinz Company
1888	Harry starts the H. J. Heinz Company
1894	Sarah Heinz dies
1906	The Pure Food and Drug Act becomes a law in the USA
1913	Harry starts work on a centre for poor children
14 May 1919	H. J. Heinz dies at the age of 75

Glossary

brickyard place where clay bricks are made and dried

chemical something added to a food to change it in some way

employee someone who works for a company

factory place where machines are used to make things

greenhouse building in which plants are grown

government group that makes laws and decisions for a country

horseradish long root vegetable that is grated and mixed with vinegar to make a spicy sauce

manager someone who is in charge of other workers in a business

marketing ways to sell a product or idea

museum place where people can see and learn about objects from the past and present

nutritious healthy and safe to eat

process to prepare and package to eat

product something that a company makes to sell

More books to read

Look After Yourself: Heathly Food, Angela Royston (Heinemann Library, 2003)

Safe and Sound: Eat Well, Angela Royston (Heinemann Library, 2000)

Index

Allegheny, Pennsylvania 14
Anchor Brand Foods 11, 12, 30

Birmingham, Pennsylvania 6
bottles 4, 9, 11
brickyard 6, 7, 10

chemicals 18, 31
children 26, 27

employees 14–15

factory 14–15, 21, 22, 24, 30, 31
farmers 17

garden 7, 15, 30
Greenfield Village 28

H. J. Heinz Company 13, 29, 30

'Heinz 57 Varieties' 21
Heinz Ocean Pier 30
Heinz, Sarah Young 12, 25, 30
horseradish 8–9, 11, 31
horses 8, 29, 30

marketing 20–21, 31
museum 23, 28, 31

nutritious food 5, 16–17, 31

pickle badge 20, 30
Pittsburgh, Pennsylvania 8, 22, 23, 24, 28
processed food 4–5, 16–17, 18, 19, 31
Pure Food and Drug Act 19, 30

Sarah Heinz House 25
Sharpsburg, Pennsylvania 6, 11, 25, 28